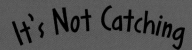

It's Not Catching

Tooth Decay

Heinemann Library
Chicago, Illinois

Angela Royston

Designed by Dave Oakley, Arnos Design
Artwork by Nick Hawken and Tower Designs UK
Originated by Dot Gradations Ltd.
Printed and bound in China
by South China Printing Company

08 07 06 05 04
10 9 8 7 6 5 4 3 2 1

Library of Congress
Cataloging-in-Publication Data
Royston, Angela.
  It's not catching tooth decay / Angela Royston.
    v. cm.
Includes bibliographical references and index.
Contents: What is tooth decay? -- Who gets tooth
decay? -- What causes tooth decay? -- How sugar
causes tooth decay -- Gum disease -- Severe
toothache -- Treating tooth decay -- Treating gum
disease -- Cleaning your teeth -- Brushing your
teeth -- Healthy food -- Fluoride -- Dental
checkups. ISBN 1-4034-4827-2 (hbk.)
  1. Dental caries--Juvenile literature. 2. Dental
caries--Prevention--Juvenile literature. [1. Teeth--
Care and hygiene.] I. Title: Tooth decay. II. Title.
  RK331.R69 2004
  617.6'7--dc22
                                        2003019820

Acknowledgments
The author and publishers are grateful to the
following for permission to reproduce copyright
material: p. 4 Getty Images/Dave Nagel; p. 5
SPL/BSIP; pp. 6, 22, 23, 24, 27 Trevor Clifford; p. 7
Eyewire; pp. 8, 9, 18, 19, 20, 21, 25 Phillip James
Photography; p. 10 SPL; p. 12 SPL/CNRI; p. 13
Gareth Boden; p. 14 SPL/BSIP/VEM; p. 16
SPL/James King-Holmes; p. 17 Powerstock/Oote
Boe; p. 26 Powerstock; p. 28 Getty Images/Jon
Riley; p. 29 Bananastock.

Cover photograph reproduced with permission of
Tudor Photography.

The publishers would like to thank David Wright
for his assistance in the preparation of this book.

Every effort has been made to contact copyright
holders of any material reproduced in this book.
Any omissions will be rectified in subsequent
printings if notice is given to the publisher.

Contents

Some words are shown in bold, **like this.** You can find out what they mean by looking in the glossary.

What Is Tooth Decay?

Healthy teeth are covered with a hard coating called **enamel.** Tooth **decay** begins when you get a small hole in the enamel on one of your teeth.

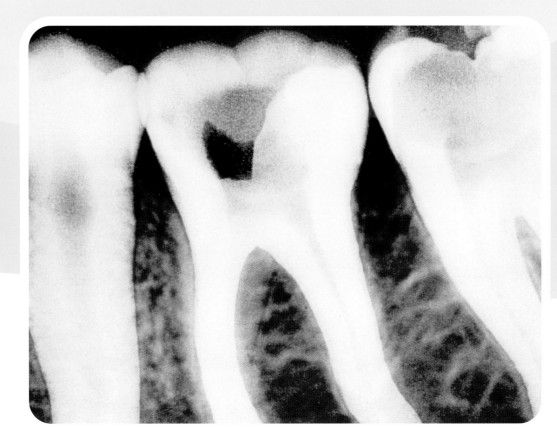

You may not feel anything until the hole becomes deeper. If the hole reaches the middle of your tooth, you may feel a painful toothache.

Who Gets Tooth Decay?

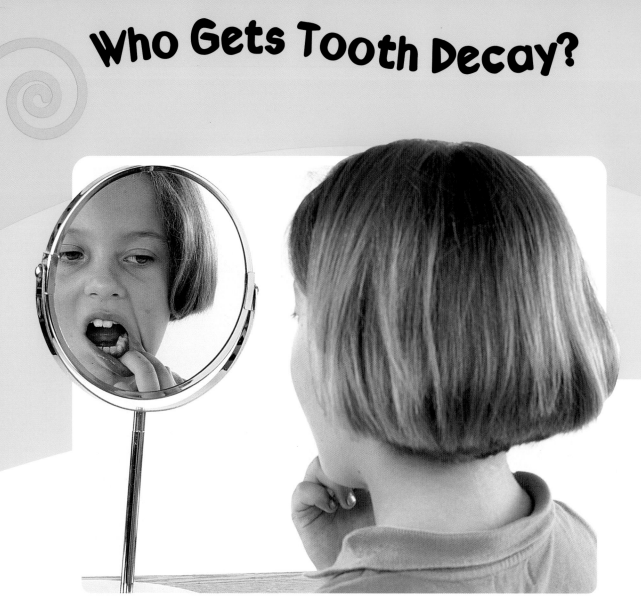

Anyone can get tooth **decay.** You cannot catch tooth decay from someone else.

You may get tooth decay if you do not take care of your teeth. People who eat and drink many sweet things are likely to get tooth decay.

What Causes Tooth Decay?

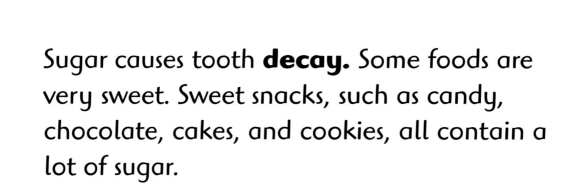

Sugar causes tooth **decay.** Some foods are very sweet. Sweet snacks, such as candy, chocolate, cakes, and cookies, all contain a lot of sugar.

Drinks such as lemonade and soda contain a lot of sugar, too. When you eat or drink sugary things, some of the sugar stays in your mouth.

Sugar Causes Tooth Decay

bacteria seen through
a microscope

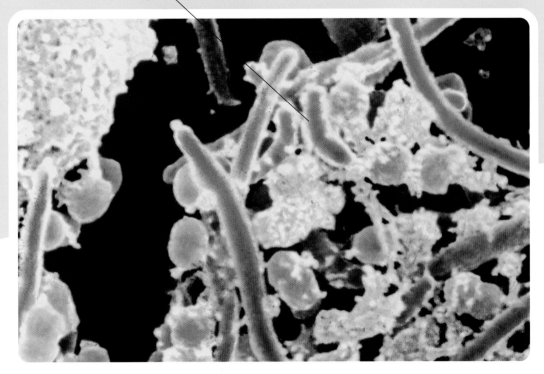

Millions of tiny **bacteria** live in your mouth.
They are too small to see except through a
microscope. The bacteria feed on the sugar
left in your mouth.

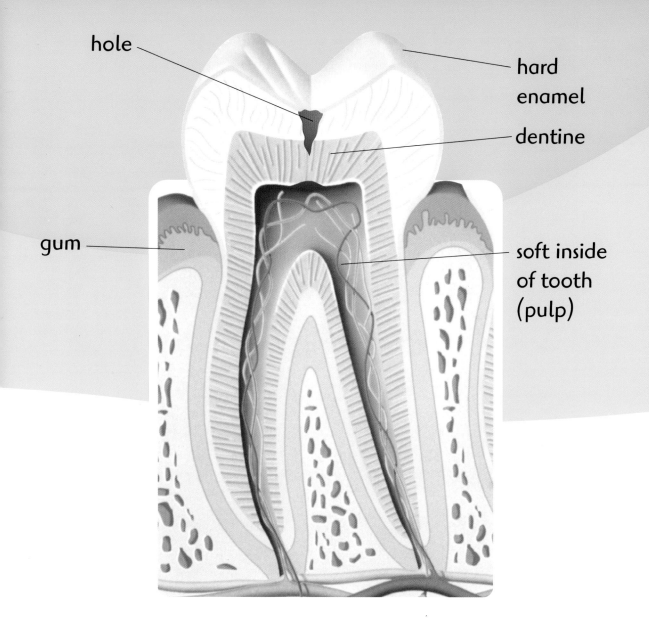

hole

hard
enamel

dentine

gum

soft inside
of tooth
(pulp)

As bacteria feeds, they produce an **acid.**
The acid burns holes in the **enamel** covering
your teeth. The acid then begins to destroy
the **dentine** below.

plaque

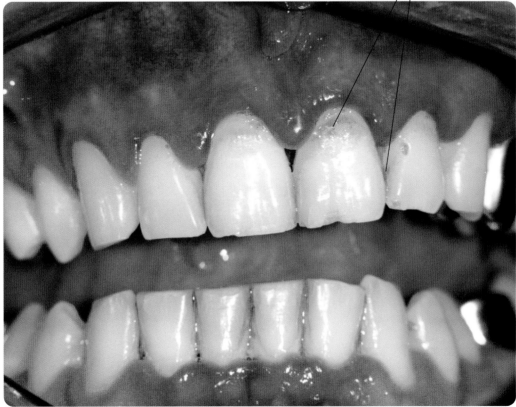

Bacteria and sugary food form a sticky paste called **plaque.** Plaque gets trapped between your teeth and your **gums.** It can also build up between your teeth.

The bacteria in plaque attacks your teeth and can **irritate** your gums. Sore gums bleed easily. Bacteria that gets under your gums can form a painful **abscess.**

Bad Toothaches

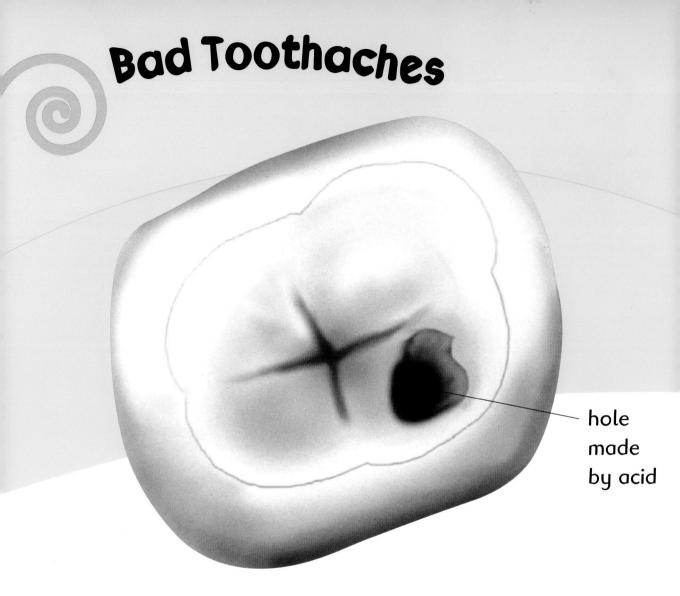

hole
made
by acid

Dentine is not as strong as the **enamel** that covers each tooth. The **acid** that causes tooth **decay** can eat its way through dentine to the **pulp.**

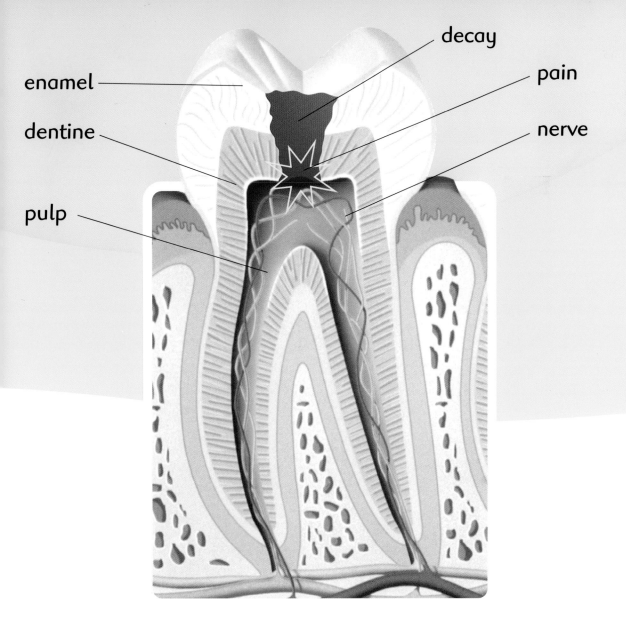

enamel

dentine

pulp

decay

pain

nerve

The pulp in the center of the tooth contains nerves and blood. As the hole gets deeper, it can cause a painful toothache. The pain tells you that something is wrong.

Treating Tooth Decay

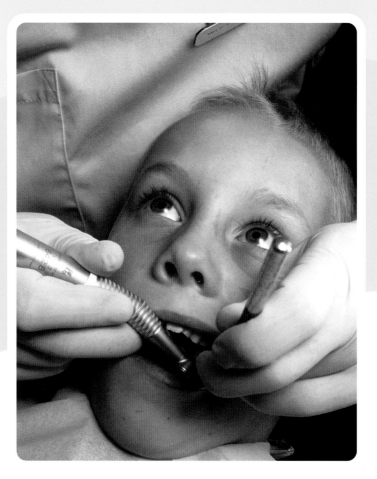

A **dentist** will treat your tooth **decay.**
First, the dentist will give you an **anesthetic**
so that you do not feel anything. Dentists
use a **drill** to get rid of all the decay in
your tooth.

filling

When the dentist is done drilling, your tooth has a much bigger hole! The dentist fills the hole with a mixture of special chemicals called a **filling.** Now the tooth is healthy again.

Treating Gum Disease

One way to get rid of **gum disease** is to rinse your mouth with **antiseptic** mouthwash. You have to rinse your mouth with mouthwash for a few minutes in the morning and again at night.

People who have an **abscess** have to
take an **antibiotic** medicine. The medicine
kills the **germs** that caused the **infection.**
The **dentist** may have to take the infected
tooth out.

Cleaning Your Teeth

Brushing your teeth helps to prevent tooth **decay.** You should brush your teeth in the morning, after every meal, and before you go to bed at night. Use toothpaste and a toothbrush.

Dental floss is a thin string that helps to get rid of **plaque** between your teeth. Your **dentist** will show you how to use floss to clean between your teeth and **gums.**

Brushing Your Teeth

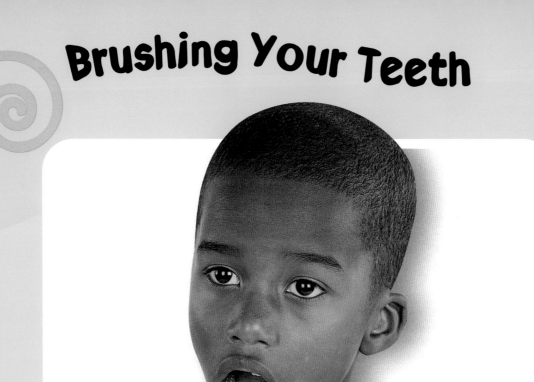

Brush each tooth from top to bottom. Brush the back of each tooth as well as the front. Then brush the tops of your back teeth.

A toothbrush only lasts for a few months. Then the bristles become soft and spread out, like this. An old toothbrush will not clean your teeth properly.

Healthy Food

Some foods help to make your teeth strong and healthy. Eating raw carrots, celery, and apples helps to clean your teeth. They are also much healthier than candy and cookies!

Milk, cheese, and yogurt contain a substance called **calcium.** Your teeth contain calcium, too. Eating calcium keeps your teeth extra strong.

Fluoride

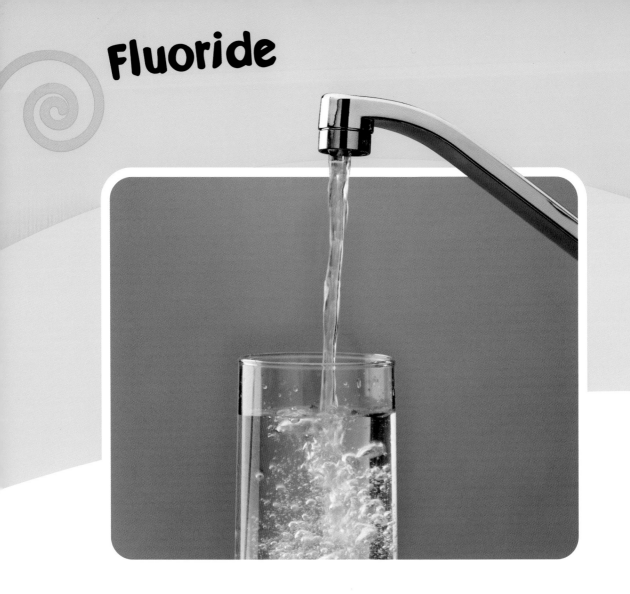

Fluoride also keeps your teeth strong so that they are much less likely to **decay.** In some places, a small amount of fluoride is added to tap water.

If your tap water has no fluoride, you can find fluoride in drops, tablets, mouthwash, or toothpaste. Ask your **dentist** if you should use extra fluoride. Too much fluoride can create white spots on your teeth.

Dental Check-ups

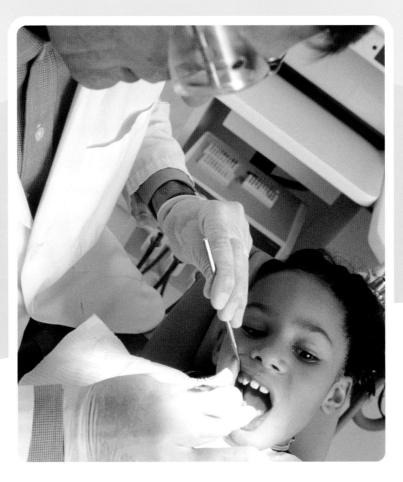

You should visit the **dentist** every six months to have your teeth checked. The dentist looks at your teeth to see if there is any tooth **decay** or **gum disease.**

The dentist may coat your teeth with a **sealant** to help stop decay. Taking care of your teeth is very important. They have to last your whole life!

Glossary

abscess   part of the skin or gums that is swollen and sore because it is infected by germs

acid   bitter or sour liquid that can burn holes in teeth

anesthetic   something that makes you lose all feeling, particularly the feeling of pain

antibiotic   medicine that cures infections caused by bacteria

antiseptic   something that stops bacteria from growing

bacteria   type of germ

calcium   mineral that makes your teeth and bones strong and hard

decay   rotten

dental floss   special thread that you use between your teeth and gums to get rid of plaque

dentine   hard part of the tooth below the enamel

dentist   person who is trained to take care of teeth

drill   instrument for making holes

enamel   very hard, shiny substance that covers the surface of a tooth

filling   chemicals that are used to fill holes in teeth

fluoride   mineral that makes your teeth healthy

germs   tiny living things, such as bacteria, that can cause sickness if they get inside your body

gum disease   sickness that makes your gums bleed

gums   skin that covers your jaw bones and the roots of your teeth

infection   sickness caused by germs

irritate   make sore

microscope   instrument that makes very small things look big enough to see

plaque   sticky paste that builds up between your teeth and under your gums

pulp   soft substance at the center of a tooth

sealant   substance that makes something airtight and watertight

More Books to Read

Royston, Angela. *Healthy Teeth.* Chicago: Heinemann Library, 2003.

Royston, Angela. *Why Do I Get a Toothache?: And Other Questions About Nerves.* Chicago: Heinemann Library, 2002.

Index